A Chance To Live

A Guide for Victims of Domestic Violence

By

Zohra Sarwari

Eman Publishing
P.O. Box 404
FISHERS, IN 46038
www.emanpublishing.com

Order Online: www.zohrasarwari.com

ISBN 13: 978-0-9841275-5-9
ISBN 10: 0-9841275-5-0
LCCN: 2010928751

EMAN
publishing

Cover Design by Madeeha Shaikh

Printed in the United States of America

Introduction

Battered Women – Begin Healing!

"The best among you is the one who is best towards his wife."
Prophet Muhammad (PBUH)

If you have ever experienced domestic violence, I don't have to tell you that it is an isolating experience. Perhaps nothing is quite as tragic as finding out that a person you thought loved you was actually more in love with the idea of controlling you in ways that are not appropriate. Even worse, the mainstream view of domestic violence ranges from 'Why doesn't she just leave?' to 'She must have done something to deserve it.'

Other than the occasional TV movie or magazine article, domestic violence seems to slip under the radar. Deep down everyone knows that it happens, but very few take the time to talk about it; and even less work to prevent it.

As a motivational speaker, I regularly hear from women who are either trapped in a violent relationship or who broke free and are struggling to find solid ground. I don't want to simply pay lip service to these women. Rather than pat them on the back and send them on their way, I wanted to provide a resource that they could turn to for encouragement and support time and time again. It was out of this desire that this book was born.

With so many books for battered women, I wanted this one to be somewhat different. I wanted my book to allow them to experience 'foreseeing the future,' by the Will of Allaah (God). By foreseeing the future, I mean that they see themselves out of their horrible situation and in a situation ten times better…all by the Will of (Allaah) God!

You see, this book was written for all of the women out there who feel that life can't get any better. It is for all the women out there who feel that they can't win, no matter how hard they try. It's for all the women out there who feel that it is entirely their fault that they are battered; and let me tell you, it is not! It's for all the women out there who just want to be happy.

This book offers a combination of motivation and support resources that can help you lead the life you've been meaning to live. So many resources for battered women focus solely on the decision to leave. However, if you've been in an abusive relationship for any period of time, you need comprehensive help to get back on your feet after you've left your abuser.

In this book you will find many examples of how you can be happy after you have made the decision to leave. The decision is difficult, but learning the skills necessary to avoid falling back into the same trap can be even harder.

Throughout this book, I will discuss the essential skills you need to survive and even thrive after leaving an abusive relationship. The information included here will cover everything from actions to take immediately after leaving, to living skills such as budgeting, to developing the self-confidence to control your future destiny. Each chapter has been specially developed with the needs of battered women in mind.

At the end of each chapter is a "Putting It into Action" section. This summary page reviews the main points of each chapter and provides a checklist. These action plans are designed to help you break free from your abusive relationship and begin the life you so truly deserve.

In addition, throughout the book are stories of other women who have broken free from the abuse they endured. While based on real stories, they have been fictionalized to protect the identity of those involved. All the stories are inspiring reminders of the strength of a woman even in the face of adversity.

I pray that every woman who reads this book will be empowered because of it, and I pray that they take action to improve their lives. More than anything I pray that (Allaah) God accepts this work from me.

"We need 4 hugs a day for survival.
We need 8 hugs a day for maintenance.
We need 12 hugs a day for growth."
Virginia Satir

Table of Contents

Chapter 1:   Break Free   8

Chapter 2:   Avoid the Cycle of Abuse   16

Chapter 3:   Cultivate Confidence   26

Chapter 4:   Nurture Self-Esteem   38

Chapter 5:   Set Goals   48

Chapter 6:   Live on a Budget   56

Chapter 7:   Manage Your Time   70

Chapter 8:   Live Your Life to The Fullest!   80

Chapter 1

Break Free

"The world is delightful, and its greatest treasure is a good woman."

Prophet Muhammad (PBUH)

For Jenny, physical abuse was a way of life. She couldn't envision a marriage any other way. The hitting, kicking, choking, and screaming were all part of her daily life.

If it hadn't been for her children, Jenny would probably still be there today...being told that she was worthless, ugly, incompetent. She had heard it so often that she believed it all.

But when she saw the bruise on her 5 year old daughter's arm, things changed. Jenny couldn't break free for herself, but she could for her daughter. The day she realized that her husband had hit their child was the day she decided to leave.

Like most abusive relationships, Jenny's marriage didn't start abusive. Her husband was a bit controlling while dating, but Jenny thought it was just a "guy thing." It was slightly cute and endearing how he became upset when another man looked at her.

It didn't take long for his scowls to turn into physical abuse. Jenny was told that men looked at her because she dressed like a 'slut.' Her husband forbade her from leaving the house without him, and beatings would occur any time he thought she had disobeyed him.

When she did leave the house, Jenny wore sunglasses to hide her black eyes. She didn't have any friends or family nearby so no one knew the truth about what was happening at home.

It wasn't until she saw the bruise on her daughter that she felt strong enough to run away from her husband. He had threatened to kill her before, and Jenny called the

Domestic Violence Hotline from a store payphone one day. They put her in touch with a local shelter that coordinated her escape.

One day, after her husband had left for work, Jenny and her daughter were picked up by a shelter volunteer. They arranged for her to spend some time in the shelter while they looked for more permanent housing.

Jenny joined a local church group and Al-Anon for support. The shelter helped her apply for a restraining order against her husband. Throughout all this, Jenny realized that she didn't need someone else to tell her she was worthy of love. She learned to value herself for who she was.

Her husband did not take the divorce well. He stalked Jenny for years, and she learned self-defense and put the police department's phone number on her cell phone's speed dial. Jenny's husband sent notes apologizing and begging for a second chance, but Jenny knew better.

She raised her daughter as a single mom, and Jenny has no regrets about her decision to leave her abusive husband. 'My only regret is not doing it earlier,' she said.

Today, Jenny is married to a man who treats her with the dignity and respect she deserves.

I hope that you have already made the decision to leave your abuser. After all, you deserve so much more than the life you are living! You are a wonderful creation made by Allaah (God) and no one has the right to treat you like a piece of property.

If you are getting ready to leave, you can call the National Domestic Violence Hotline at 1-800-799-SAFE (7233). They have advocates available 24 hours a day, 365 days a year. Not only can they help you formulate an escape plan, but they can also put you in contact with local women's resource shelters that provide temporary housing and other services. All calls are 100% private and confidential. *I urge you to call TODAY if you are in an abusive relationship.*

After You Leave

There are special considerations to take when leaving an abusive relationship. Don't make the mistake of thinking that the relationship ends when you walk out of the door. Abusers are not rational people; when they lose control of someone, they often become either enraged or desperate to win you back. That means that ending the relationship is going to require extra steps and time.

I know that sounds overwhelming. You want to be out and out now! However, your safety and that of your children is most important. Take the time to make sure you are protected while you break free. The following 3 steps are vital:

1.) **Get a Restraining Order:** This is important no matter how 'minor' the abuse may have seemed. You have no idea how your abuser is going to respond so it is vital to be prepared. Even if they violate the order, the local prosecutor can then take steps to put him behind bars and assure your safety. Keep a certified copy of the court order with you at all times and don't hesitate to call 911 if your ex gets too close for comfort.

2.) **Make Changes on the Home Front:** If you are able to stay in your home, it is important to change up your routine. It goes without saying that you should change the locks on the house. Consider switching your phone number as well.

Then, make sure you change your route to school or work. Being unpredictable makes you less vulnerable to an angry ex.

3.) **Let Others Know:** Okay, I know it can be embarrassing to admit to others what is going on; but at the very least you need to inform your kids' school. Abusers often target children and pets, and the school has to know to watch out for your ex. You should also let friends know about your situation so they can offer support; and, if you are close to your neighbors, they can also help by keeping an eye on your house while you are gone. Sure, it is difficult to ask for help, but remember: there is safety in numbers. That's why your abuser has tried so hard to cut you off from everyone else.

The Definition of Abuse

If you haven't yet left your partner, you may be wondering at what point bad behavior is considered abuse. I can certainly understand that marriage vows are 'for better or for worse,' but almost any spiritual leader would tell you that abuse cannot be tolerated.

Some of the common forms of abuse include:

   o **Physical Abuse:** This is the type of abuse we most often associate with domestic violence. It may include slapping, punching, pinching, biting, pushing or throwing objects during an argument. Physical abuse may extend to children and pets in the house as well. With few exceptions, physical abuse is almost universally accepted as a valid reason to leave a relationship.

o **Verbal Abuse:** Many domestic violence survivors say that the verbal abuse they endured was the most damaging part of their relationship. Abusers use verbal abuse to manipulate and control their partners. They continually tell them that they are ugly and stupid until they begin to believe the lies. They blame problems on the victim and isolate their partners from family and friends. Verbal abuse often extends to children in the household as well.

o **Financial Abuse:** Less recognized is financial abuse. This is where an abuser uses financial power to hold his victim captive. He may insist you quit your business. He will cut you off from the bank accounts and take away your car key. In essence, he makes you helpless and dependent on him.

If you are unsure whether your partner's behavior rises to the level of abuse, it may help to have a trial separation to sort out your feelings. Taking a step back from the situation will help you understand more clearly if your husband is battling a problem such as depression or is verbally abusing you.

Warning: If your partner has ever physically abused you or threatened to hurt you if you try to leave, do NOT tell him that you want a separation while you are still in the house. Call the Domestic Violence Hotline 1-800-799-SAFE (7233) and get to a safe place before informing your spouse. Then, contact an attorney and have the attorney deliver the news. The announcement of a separation can easily throw physically violent individuals over the edge, and you do not want to be around this person when they find out you are leaving.

Another way to sort out abuse from other issues such as poor communication skills is to suggest counseling. A good counselor will be able to help you determine whether your spouse is abusive or just needs some relationship skills. If your husband refuses to go to counseling, go by yourself.

Sometimes, all it takes is the suggestion that the marriage needs help to determine whether your husband is abusive. Overall, husbands who love their wives will be willing to work on improving the marriage. Abusive spouses, on the other hand, will become angry and defensive at the thought of outside interference in their relationship. After all, they are more interested in controlling you than loving you; and a counselor most definitely threatens their control.

"The fastest way to change society is to mobilize the women of the world."
Charles Malik

Putting It into Action

___ If you haven't left yet, create a list of items you have access to that you can take with you. Don't forget important documents such as account statements, birth certificates, social security cards etc.

___ Call the National Domestic Violence Hotline: 1-800-799-SAFE (7233), to find a women's shelter in your area.

___ Pack a bag and determine a time when your abuser will be gone and you can safely leave.

___ Make arrangements in advance with a shelter or other safe place to stay.

___ File for a restraining order.

___ If your abuser agrees to leave and you return to the house, change the locks.

___ Find a support group or enlist friends who can help you with the transition out of the relationship.

Chapter 2

Avoid the Cycle of Abuse

"To live a life of happiness, you must do what's right."
Zohra Sarwari

I am a 5 year survivor of domestic abuse. It was 5 years ago that I walked out of the door, and I haven't been back since. I may be single, but I live life on my own terms now. I don't miss the abuse; I don't miss the swearing. I have full custody of our son so I have no reason to even talk to him.

When I got pregnant, he started slapping me around. I should have known better then…I think probably every domestic abuse survivor says that. He made cracks about me being barefoot and pregnant cooking dinner, I would get annoyed and then he would punch me.

I thought it might be pregnancy hormones that were making me unreasonable, but it got worse after the baby was born. My husband told me over and over 'You ain't nobody' and 'You can leave me…what ya going to do, live on the street with a baby?'

The verbal abuse continued every single day, but he only hit me when he was drunk. He started drinking more and more so the physical abuse escalated.

While I was pregnant, he forbade me from having a baby shower. I was going to college, and he forced me to drop out.

My hair, my clothes, my shoes – everything was his doing. It was like I was his Barbie doll. He took my paycheck, deposited it and never gave me a cent. I couldn't even tell you how much I made.

I tried to make things right for about a year, but nothing I did helped. Finally, I decided he was the problem, not me. It took me about 3 months after coming to that conclusion before I finally worked up the courage to leave. I contacted an old college professor I trusted and explained my situation. She helped me find a shelter to stay in when I left.

I'll always remember that last look at the house before I left. I promised myself I was never going back, and I haven't. Someday, I'd like to be married again to a nice man that doesn't drink or smoke. But in the meantime, I am happy with it being just me and my son.

Staying in the shelter that first night was tough, but it was worth it. If you are with a man who makes you feel worthless, RUN! I used to think my husband would change, but now I know better. Abusers never change. Get out while you can!

You would think that once you've been in an abusive relationship it would be easy to avoid landing in the same spot again. Wrong! The number of women who go from one abusive relationship to another is appalling.

There are a number of reasons why women trade one bad relationship for another. It may be low-self esteem – the belief that they simply can't do any better. It may be money – insecurity in finances that makes them settle for the first guy who can pay the bills. It may be an extension of their family experience – their father beat their mother so they believe that's just how relationships go.

In this book, I strive to address each of these issues. I hope to make you feel confident enough in yourself and your self-worth that you never again settle for an abusive man. In the meantime, let's look at the warning signs of abuse so you can identify the red flags as soon as they go up.

When Love is Not Really Love

Initially, abusers can come across as real Romeos; they may show up at work every day with flowers. Or they may call you 10 times a day to say they love you. It all seems sweet and sincere until it begins to feel slightly suffocating. When you tell an abuser how you feel, they will put it back on you. Obviously, there is something wrong with you. They may say that you don't know how to let someone treat you well or that they are just trying to be kind while you are uncaring.

Don't be fooled – the abuser isn't trying to love you. They are trying to control you. They can also be insanely jealous of anything else that may take your time away from them. They don't show up at work with flowers because they want to say 'I love you'; they are doing it to check up on you.

Personality Traits of Abusers

Individuals who abuse others often share many of the same personality traits. While one or two of these alone may be character flaws, they can also signal a deeper problem. If you marry someone who exhibits these issues, it may be time to step back and re-evaluate whether they are a safe and healthy partner for you.

- **High Expectations** – Many abusers will not only put you on a pedestal, but also expect you to live up to their unreal expectations. You will need to keep the house clean, be beautiful and not to mention a fabulous romantic partner; anything less will be completely unacceptable.

- **Defensive** – An abuser is never wrong. It is always your fault. If they forget to pick up dinner ingredients, it is because you didn't call to remind them. If they lose their temper, it's because of something you said. Even in situations where the blame is obvious – such as getting a speeding ticket – it will be shifted to others. Of course, in their eyes it is obvious – obvious that the police are out to get them!

- **Sensitive** - Along with being defensive, individuals prone to abuse can be highly sensitive. They are easily 'hurt' by anyone questioning their motives or actions. Any criticism, no matter how constructive, is received as a scathing personal attack.

- **Moody** - It is often said that abusive individuals seem to have split personalities. They are happy and kind one moment and fly into a rage the next. Sometimes this can be caused by mental illness, but it is also a result of immaturity and hypersensitivity. In addition, victims of domestic violence often have to contend with disbelief from friends and family. That's because it is not uncommon for abusers to wear a mask in public; one that makes them look like the perfect partner. They may go to church, participate in school events and otherwise play the part of a wonderful, selfless person; when the mask comes off at home, only their immediate family sees their true nature.

- **Poor Attitude Towards Women** – Many men who abuse have a negative attitude towards women. These views make you not an equal partner in a relationship, but a subservient being unworthy of respect. Now, if your partner seems to dismiss you and your opinions as inferior, you may want to consider getting counseling help.

- **Poor Communication Skills** – In an ideal relationship, both partners would sit down and calmly discuss their differences and come to a rational compromise. However, getting an abuser to even sit and talk is a feat in and of itself. When an abuser becomes angry or upset, he may mope around the house for days before telling you the problem. Instead of opening up and discussing his thoughts and feelings, he expects you to magically know the problem and then fix it.

Progression of an Abusive Relationship

While every situation is unique, it is rare that a relationship is abusive right from the start. Usually, a relationship starts off as normal, but before jumping into a relationship with someone; consider whether the following applies to your new suitor. Alone, one trait may just be a character flaw; however, if your new relationship shows signs of the following progression, tread very carefully:

Insecurity: Your new husband *needs* you. He reminds you of this on a daily basis. You are the sun, and his world revolves around you. If you were ever to leave him, he doesn't know what he would do. He might even threaten to hurt himself. Being so wanted can be flattering at first, but it is also a trademark of abusers. Their insecurity leads to jealousy, control issues and more.

Jealousy: As stated above, along with insecurity comes jealousy. An abuser might start out by playfully asking you where you've been, what you've been doing and who you've talked to. If you object to the third degree questioning, your husband will remind you that they only ask because they love you **so** much. However, all that jealousy will get old quickly and soon lead to controlling behavior.

Controlling: Soon you will find that your new partner is making demands of you. They aren't comfortable with you speaking to certain people. They would rather you come straight home from work. They think your mother doesn't like them and want to skip family events. Soon their requests turn into demands and maybe you decided it is easier to do what they ask instead of fight about it every night. Be careful! This is where abusers cut you off from everyone and make it increasingly difficult for you to escape.

Isolating: At this point, the abuser begins to cut you off from all your friends and family. It is often such a gradual process that you don't realize it is happening. Soon, you will spend all your time with your husband and no one else. He may even insist that you quit your job and stay home. If your friends and family begin commenting that they never see you anymore, it could be that your husband is working to isolate you.

Red Flags – Turn and Run!

All the above traits are common in abusive relationships. If your partner exhibits any of these, it is time for some serious re-evaluation regarding whether this person is healthy for you. At the very least, you must insist on some counseling both individually and as a couple before becoming any more seriously involved in this relationship. Even if you decide that your loved one merely has some personality flaws, all the above issues are serious enough to require intervention – both for his sake as well as yours.

However, there are red flags that can never be ignored or played down. These are make-or-break issues and you should **never** be in a relationship with someone who exhibits any of the following: don't walk away – run!

The following are red flags that should signal that it is time to end the relationship:

> **Cruelty to Animals** – Abusers often start with the most helpless creatures they can find. Know that someone who is mean to animals today may be cruel to you tomorrow.

> **Cruelty to Children** – This one really doesn't even warrant an explanation. Do you really want to be with someone who is cruel to children?

> **Past Battering Behavior** – Anyone who has battered a woman in the past should not be considered husband material...especially if he tells you that it won't happen again because 'You're different.' Even in cases where you think he's changed, don't risk it; your life is worth more than giving someone a second chance.

> **Threats of Violence** – This doesn't just mean threats against you. Anyone who makes statements about how they want to hurt or punish others is not deserving of being in a relationship with you.

> **Verbal Abuse/Name-Calling** – It doesn't matter if he only said it was because he was angry or having a bad day. Someone who calls you names, tells you that you're worthless or otherwise makes you feel bad doesn't truly love you. Get out before the abuse turns violent.

> **Drug or Alcohol Abuse** – Drug and alcohol abuse doesn't necessarily mean a person will be abusive, but it most certainly brings a whole host of problems to a relationship; problems you are better off without.

- ➢ **Destroying Objects/Treasured Items** – Abusers may want to punish you: punish you by breaking something you love. If it's only your Grandmother's china that got smashed, count yourself fortunate that you saw his true colors before he became physically violent with you.

- ➢ **Badgering/Restraining Behavior During an Argument** – If you need space during an argument, an abuser may follow you until you concede the point to him. He may also use physical force to restrain you or stop you from leaving.

Perhaps the biggest trap women fall into is hoping that they can change their partner. They say, 'He is a great guy, **except**...' To the women I counsel, I ask, *'Except that he beats you twice a month? Does that sound like someone who is great?'*

Maybe he does have fabulous potential other than the fact that he requires a detailed list of everything you've done during the day. If letting go of his control issues is his only flaw, fine. Let him go and fix that problem on his own and then come back to you.

It is not your job to fix him. And it is not your job to stay in an unhealthy relationship and convince him he needs to address his control issues. Unless he is willing to make changes, you need to come to terms with the fact that he really isn't much of a catch and there are a whole lot of better fish out in the sea.

"People with clenched fists cannot shake hands."
Indira Gandhi

Putting It into Action

___ Think about your abusive relationship. What was the first sign of trouble? Why did you ignore those early warning signs?

___ Consider why you feel like you need to be in a relationship. Is there something lacking in your life that makes you prone to staying in a bad relationship just for the sake of being in a relationship?

___ Schedule therapy sessions; these can help you heal from your previous relationship and gain insight to avoid unhealthy partnerships in the future.

___ Surround yourself with loving and supportive people.

___ Enter into a future relationship slowly. Make sure that you do a background check on him.

Chapter 3

Cultivate Confidence

"To be strong, you must have a purpose."
Zohra Sarwari

It took nearly 15 years before Georgia was willing to leave her husband. At first she thought that her new husband was being sweet and protective. Later, she told herself that he was just quirky. Finally, she could not deny that something had gone horribly wrong in her marriage.

Each morning, her husband would walk her to her car and write down the odometer number. Each night, he would do the same. He long ago made her quit her job as a nurse at the local med center and insisted that she get permission before going anywhere. If the odometer showed she had made an unapproved trip, she could expect a verbal dressing down at best or a beating at worst.

Despite hoping and praying for years that the situation would improve, it never did. Her husband's anger seemed to escalate, and his fuse became shorter and shorter. One day, while watching an afternoon talk show, it finally all clicked. "They were talking about domestic violence," Georgia recalls. "And all of a sudden, it dawned on me. They were talking about me."

That same day, Georgia began to make her plan. Her husband always took the phone to work with him so she had no way to call the local women's shelter beforehand. However, she spent the next week gathering up important information and paperwork and packed up what she could fit in the car. Everything else, she left behind.

When the day came, Georgia drove to school and picked up her three kids so they would be with her and drove to a pay phone. She called the local shelter and made arrangements for a place to stay that night. The staff at the shelter helped her file for a PPO the next day and start divorce proceedings. They also helped her find a job and a permanent place to call her own.

Georgia has a lot to be thankful for. She is most grateful for her children and that she can now stand proud and be a role model of strength and independence.

One of the keys to avoiding the trap of abuse is to increase your confidence. Abusers are master manipulators who prey on women with little faith in their own abilities. They look for women searching for a white knight and swoop in to fill that role. Once they have convinced you that you need them, the abuse begins.

Not only does increasing your self-confidence make you less likely to attract the type of men who may be abusive, it also puts you in a state of mind that says, 'I don't need to compromise my self-worth for someone else.' Self-confidence is both empowering and liberating, and something every woman should work to cultivate.

Confidence Comes From Within

I probably don't have to tell you that confidence can only be found inside yourself. It would be nice if it was bottled up and you could find it on the supermarket shelf, but it just doesn't work that way. No, confidence comes from you, and you alone.

Unfortunately, this sometimes gives people the impression that confidence is one of those traits that can't be developed. Unless you were one of the fortunate few who are born naturally self-confident, you might have to work on it. Although it is true that some women have a natural tendency towards confidence, there is simply no reason why you too can't become a strong, confident woman.

So the question is how do you create confidence? Let me tell you, it isn't something that can be learned by reading a book. You can be motivated to be self-confident and you can be inspired to be self-confident. However, you will only truly *be* self-confident once you start practicing it.

In this chapter, we'll look at some of the steps you can take to cultivate confidence in your life. Remember that you will not feel self-confident overnight. This is especially true if you have been in an abusive relationship. Your abuser has done everything in his power to beat you down, make you feel worthless and destroy your confidence. It will take time to return to a place where you can feel good about who you are and what you can accomplish.

However, I urge you to take the first step today. Read on to get started…

Define Yourself

Before you can be confident in whom you are you need to seriously evaluate yourself. Chances are your abuser has been the one to define you in the past. He probably put you in a box so to speak and dictated what you could or could not do. Maybe he defined you as the mother of his children or the maid.

Well, I have news for you! He is out of your life and can no longer tell you what you can and cannot do. You call the shots now!

When you think about defining yourself, I want you to ignore the past messages you received from your abuser or maybe society in general about your role in life. The process of self-discovery can take time so try not to rush it. You may need to spend weeks or even months mulling over who you truly are.

But to start, find a quiet place where you will not be distracted or interrupted. Have a journal or notebook with you. Sit in a comfortable place and close your eyes. Now breathe deeply and relax. It's time to think about whom you are and your place in the world.

As you work to define yourself, think about the answers to the following questions:

- What moment in your life gives you the most pride?
- If money or time were not an object, what would you like to be doing in your life right now?
- What does your perfect day look like?
- Are there any hobbies or activities you currently enjoy or would like to try?
- If you have children, how do you see your role in their life?
- What is your deepest passion? What fires you up and energizes you?
- What skills do you have?
- What skills do you want to obtain?
- How would you want your life to look in 5 years? 10 years?

Take notes in your journal as you think about these questions. Again, this is not going to be a half hour session and you are done. In most domestic violence situations, the victim shuts down and begins working on auto-pilot; the abuser makes all the decisions and dictates how they should live. There is no reason to be ashamed about this. It is simply a defense mechanism you used to protect yourself. However, now it is time to break free and create your own identity. Take as much time as you need until you feel that you have fully defined who you are, your core values and your life goals.

Write a Mission Statement

Once you have the answers to who you are, it is time to pull all that information together into one mission statement. You may think a mission statement is just for businesses or charities, but a personal mission statement is incredibly empowering.

A mission statement gives you focus and acts as a solid foundation upon which to make life decisions. If you are not sure whether something is a good choice for you, simply refer to your mission statement. If the new activity doesn't align with your mission, then you know it is time to say 'no thanks' and move on to other endeavors.

Again, find a time and place where you can be alone and uninterrupted. Review all your notes from when you decided to define yourself. Then pull out the key points; the ones that speak to you the most. Then, pull them together into a few sentences that you will be able to memorize.

Here's a sample mission statement:

'I am an attractive woman who is raising 3 children to be caring and compassionate individuals. I am focused on creating a new career in accounting that will meet my needs financially while my faith will sustain me emotionally and spiritually. I will work on achieving my destiny in this life and will not be pressured into meeting other people's expectations of me.'

Once you have your mission statement completed, write it on a blank piece of paper. If you have a photo or image that is of that special place that you hope to visit someday, add it to your mission statement.

Take your mission statement and place it somewhere where you will see it every morning. It could be your bathroom mirror or on the refrigerator. Just make sure it is in a location where you will be able to read it in the morning. You want your mission statement to set the tone for your whole day.

Learn New Skills

It is not uncommon for victims of domestic abuse to feel doubt in their abilities because they have never had an opportunity to learn the skills needed to succeed. You may have gotten married out of high school and skipped college or your abuser may have limited you to cleaning and cooking chores.

If you have limited skills, you can easily boost your self-confidence by expanding your knowledge. Many communities have wonderful continuing education programs. These classes may be free or offered at a nominal fee. They cover everything from computing skills, to budgeting, to career services. The beauty of them is that they attract people from all walks of life so you never have to feel like you will stick out as the only adult in a class full of college-age students.

You can also go beyond learning basic skills and experiment with different hobbies and fun activities. With a little research, you may be able to find the following events in your area:

- Cooking Classes
- Book Clubs
- Religious Classes
- Business Courses
- Guest Lectures
- Parenting Classes
- Gardening Classes

As you begin to branch out and try new activities, you will find that your confidence level will grow. In addition, you will open doors to new opportunities that can give your life a greater purpose and fulfillment.

Meet New People

One of the hallmarks of domestic violence is isolation; you most likely spent long hours at home alone. Your abuser may have told you that you are ugly, boring and incapable of making friends. Not only does that type of talk crush your self-esteem, it destroys your confidence as well. You may find that you don't want to step out of your comfort zone because you are afraid your abuser was right when he said you would fail.

However, friendships are vital not only to happiness but also to healing. A strong support network can help you move on from a painful past and avoid unhealthy relationships in the future.

If you are hesitant about dipping into the social pool again, you may want to start at a local support group for battered women. There, you know you will be surrounded by supportive people who have been where you are. They can provide friendship, support and referrals to resources you may need.

As you become more confident, you can seek out friends elsewhere as well. Community activities, religious circles, and school functions are all great places to meet like-minded individuals. Don't be afraid to go to an event alone. Promise yourself that you will stay for at least half an hour and talk to one new person – even if it is just to say 'hi' – before leaving. By mastering small feats like this, you will build confidence for the future.

Remember that you will not always become friends with every person you meet, and that is absolutely fine. If someone doesn't seem too interested, don't take it personally. With so many people in your community, it is simply a question of searching until you find the ones with whom you 'click.'

A final comment on meeting new friends: people will invariably ask about your past. It is an inevitable part of small talk. Folks inquire into your job, your marriage, and your kids. Don't feel obligated to go into your life story. If someone asks you whether you are married, a simple 'We're divorced or separated,' will suffice. If you are asked about what happened, don't feel bad saying, 'It just didn't work out,' and then changing the subject. You don't owe anyone an explanation of your past.

Set Goals and Take Risks

Using your mission statement as a guide, you can set goals for yourself. They may be lofty goals like owning a business or a house within the next five years or smaller goals such as making one new friend.

Review the notes you took while defining yourself to help you pick out a couple of goals you would like to achieve. Make sure the goals correspond to your mission statement; otherwise, you can always adjust your mission statement to reflect your new goals.

Once you have made your goals, determine what steps you need to reach them. Break these steps into manageable chunks that are realistic. For example, let's say your goal is to go on a trip. Your steps could be:

1.) Make an appointment with a career counselor.
2.) Write a resume.
3.) Apply for 5 jobs a week.
4.) Take a basic computing skills class while job searching.
5.) Once hired, put 10% of your pay aside for the trip.

6.) Plan the trip with your family!

7.) Take the trip with your family!

See how this gives you a series of small steps that will ultimately lead to your goal of traveling? Do the same for your goal, whatever it may be.

As you work towards your goal, keep in mind that sometimes you need to step outside of your comfort zone. Taking small risks and being successful can make you more confident. If you should encounter a setback when taking a risk, remind yourself that it is not a failure; it is a learning experience.

Fake It Until You Make It

Still not feeling confident? Then pretend. No one on the street will be any wiser. Hold your head up high and act how you envision confident people act. Again, no one at the restaurant, grocery store or bookstore will know any different.

If you make a mistake, trip over your feet or do anything else that makes you want to crawl under a rock and hide, think about how a confident person would handle that situation; pretend you are that person. Smile and be on your way, pretending like whatever happened doesn't make a bit of difference in your world.

Soon, you will find that you become that confident person you are pretending to be. Really! It is amazing how our mind follows our actions. Once you convince yourself that you are confident, you will be confident. It's that simple!

So start today…no more apologizing for what is out of your control; no more mumbling when talking to others.

From this day forward, act confident, and world-class confidence will be right behind you!

On the subject of confidence, I leave you with this one final thought:

"Whether you think you can or think you can't, you are right."
Henry Ford

Putting It into Practice

____ Identify your strengths and weaknesses.

____ Write a list of 5 hobbies or areas that interest you. Make it a priority to explore one area each month for the next 5 months.

____ Create a personal mission statement.

____Develop action plans for 3 goals. Remember to break each goal into attainable and measurable steps.

____ Take a risk this week; whether it is introducing yourself to someone new at the mosque, or applying for a new job, step outside your comfort zone.

Chapter 4

Nurture Self-Esteem

"Nobody can make you feel inferior without your permission."
Eleanor Roosevelt

It was love at first sight when I met my husband. I instantly fell in love with him, and I thought he loved me too. We dated for about a year, and he was perfect in every way. He spent time with my family, went to church with me and devoted every Friday as our date night. I truly felt like a queen.

After the wedding, all that started to change. He would pick fights about little things and then stop talking to me for the rest of the week. He became moody and angry if I moved his stuff without asking. Eventually, he took over the finances and started playing mind games with me.

He would always say the right thing, but his attitude would be all wrong. If I tried to call him on it, it was always pegged as me giving him a hard time. I could do nothing right in his eyes. It got to the point where I was afraid to talk to him. He would always glare at me and called me awful names when he did talk.

Then he started drinking, and things got even worse. I pleaded for him to stop, but he wouldn't. He told me that he had to drink to deal with me; that I was a pain...that he had to sacrifice everything for me and I was ungrateful. He said such hurtful things. Once, he even threatened to kill me.

This went on for years until one day I decided I had enough. I called the local shelter which helped me get out of the house. They set me up with an apartment and a new unlisted number. Life is much better now, but I still struggle. Every time I look in the mirror, I still remember all those awful names my husband called me.

Fortunately, I feel like I am finally starting to come out of that long, dark tunnel and into the daylight.

As we discussed in the last chapter, domestic violence can work to systematically destroy both your self-confidence and your self-esteem. We've discussed practical ways to boost self-confidence and let's now look at self-esteem. Before we get into how to increase self-esteem, let's first discuss what it is.

There is a drug abuse prevention program called Project Charlie. At the start of each lesson, the volunteer teaching the class writes on the board, "You are someone special." This, my friends, is the essence of self-esteem. It is the belief that you have your own unique value...one that isn't dependent on what you do or how much money you make or how talented you are. Self-esteem is knowing that you have an inner value that cannot be taken away.

What does that have to do with drug abuse prevention? You see, the Project Charlie program understands that good self-esteem is critical to making good choices. Children who don't feel good about themselves are likely to try drugs either to fit in with other kids or to escape from their worries.

As a domestic violence survivor, it is vital to understand how your self-esteem plays into your future relationships. As discussed in chapter 2, some women jump from one abusive relationship to another. Poor self-esteem is one of the biggest reasons why women allow themselves to continue in this pattern of abuse. They have decided that they are worth nothing and an abusive man is the best they can expect to get.

Low self-esteem can also have serious repercussions beyond just relationships. It can result in:

- Depression
- Anxiety
- Unhealthy Weight Gain or Loss
- Chronic Fatigue
- Insomnia

- Depressed Immune System

Women with children need to be particularly careful about the impact of low self-esteem in their families. A woman who thinks she is ugly and worthless risks raising children who feel the same way. This is particularly tragic for daughters who already have to contend with a media and culture that demands unattainable perfection from women.

Restoring Self-Esteem

Of course it is easiest if you never lose your self-esteem in the first, but it can be restored. Many of the exercises in the preceding chapter on confidence can go a long way to increasing your self-esteem; and it is no wonder since the two often go hand in hand. However, there are 3 activities that I recommend to anyone looking for increased self-esteem:

Daily Affirmations: Some folks don't like affirmations, and I can understand why. It seems a little "touchy-feely" at best and hokey at worst. After all, standing in front of a mirror saying nice things about yourself seems a bit like something a news anchor with an inflated ego might do.

Okay, so it might seem silly, but the truth about affirmations is…they really work! It is a bit like becoming confident by acting confident. After you tell yourself enough times that you are a great person, you will start to believe it.

So each day…when you first wake up and when you get ready for sleep…say one or two affirmations to yourself. These are statements of intention. For example, here are some affirmations:

- I am a beautiful person who deserves to be loved.
- I make enough money to pay my bills and meet my needs.
- I am an interesting woman, and people enjoy talking with me.
- I am smart and intelligent. I make wise choices.
- I am worthy of love.
- I deserve all that life has to offer.

See, these don't have to match your current situation. Maybe you don't make enough to pay all the bills right now. However, by making a daily commitment to that goal and phrasing it as though it were a fact, you help turn it into reality.

There is much to be said for the power of positive thinking and our subconscious minds. Daily affirmations help tap into both those resources.

Turn to Allaah (God): Almost every major world religion places emphasis on the importance and value of each individual. If you find yourself struggling with your self-worth, it may be time to look for deeper meaning in the world. Maybe it is time you asked yourself what is the purpose of life?

Explore the meaning of life and God's purpose for us on your own. There are many excellent books available from the library as well as countless websites devoted to these subjects.

Although it can be a weighty subject to delve into, you may find deep satisfaction in faith and the belief that we are all born with an intrinsic value that no human can take away.

Take Stock of Your Strengths: There is no better way to improve self-esteem than to come to the realization that you are a pretty amazing person. No matter what path you've had in life, you undoubtedly have some incredible strength.

Instead of focusing on what you cannot do, shift your inner dialogue to what you can do. If you went through a 10 year battle with an abusive husband, you can most certainly say that you are a strong woman. If you've left that abuser, you can most certainly say that you are smart woman. And if you are on the road to a better life, you can most certainly say that you are a woman with a vision.

Your strengths can also be talents such as:

- Sewing
- Writing
- Gardening
- Teaching
- Cooking
- Nurturing
- Listening
- Volunteering
- Crafting

It doesn't matter what they are; what matters is that you know that you have positive attributes. You are not the dumb, worthless woman your ex tried to convince you that you were. No, you are the woman who can make beautiful craftwork. You are the woman who is always there to lend a compassionate ear to others in need. You are the woman who is driven to make the world a better place.

How Positive Thinking Helps You

Some women don't make increasing their self-esteem a priority. They tend to think that it doesn't rank as high as budgeting or education. It is a shame that they believe this because almost every aspect of life can benefit from healthy self-esteem.

With confidence and good self-esteem, the sky can be the limit. Imagine how you would like to be perceived. Would you want others to see you as…

- •Optimistic?
- •Independent?
- •Respectable?
- •Focused?
- •Responsible?
- •Persistent?

All these are the characteristics of people who have high self-esteem. Perhaps more importantly, these are also the people who enjoy life to the fullest. They don't take it personally when the cashier doesn't smile at them or a car cuts them off on the highway; they know that these have nothing to do with what they did or did not do. Having great self-esteem means being able to spend each day focused on the positive instead of dwelling on life's little inconveniences.

In addition, those with healthy self-esteem are able to accept all the good that comes in life without feeling guilty. So many people with low self-esteem believe that they are not worthy of success or happiness. It can affect them to the point where they subconsciously try to sabotage themselves!

Self-esteem creates a sense of humor and creativity. Rather than allow yourself to be boxed in by what others expect of you, healthy self-esteem helps you create new opportunities based upon your interests and strengths.

Finally, good self-esteem lets you love others fully while accepting unconditional love in return. This is so important for victims of domestic violence to understand.

Battered women have been conditioned to believe they are not worthy of love and compassion; they are programmed to think that it must be earned. Once your self-esteem has rebounded, you can truly see when someone loves and respects you and is not just trying to use you.

"There are two ways of spreading light ...
To be the candle, or the mirror that reflects it."
Edith Wharton

Putting It into Action

____ Write a list of 5 daily affirmations. Place one on your bathroom mirror, one on the refrigerator door, one in your car and the other two by your bed stand. Say one upon waking, and one before going to bed in the evening. Say the others every time you are in the bathroom, kitchen or car.

____ Eliminate negative influences in your life. If you have friends who are negative and make you feel bad about yourself, put some distance between you and them. Make a point to surround yourself only with people and things that boost your self-esteem.

____ Consider, looking for the purpose of life in faith. Ask the Creator to help you connect with Him.

____ Replace negative thoughts with positive ones. Focus on all that is good about you.

Chapter 5

Set Goals

"You may be disappointed if you fail, but you are doomed if you don't try."
Beverly Sills

It was surprising that Tracy found herself in an abusive relationship. As a child, she was strong-willed to the point of defiance. No one was going to tell her what to do.

But when she got married, that changed. She was married young to her high school sweetheart. Deep down, she thought she would never get any other guy.

He was so jealous and angry, but Tracy didn't realize that that wasn't normal. She thought every guy was that way – it was a sign of love.

When he started hitting her, Tracy thought the same thing…maybe this is just the way marriages are. Tracy felt like the abuse was her fault and she was too embarrassed to say anything. Her husband would smother her under pillows until she stopped breathing and throw her against walls. She never had bruises that could be seen so no one realized something was wrong.

Tracy's husband was a prominent businessman who regularly told her that she was nothing compared to him. After a while, she began to believe his lies.

It wasn't until a chance encounter at the library that Tracy began to find her self-confidence. An old friend ran into her and mentioned a book by feminist Gloria Steinem. Tracy took the book out of the library and read it cover to cover that night.

A light flicked on inside her, and she realized that she was worth more than she had allowed herself to become. She returned to the library the next day and took out more books.

Rather than bow to her husband's every wish, she began to stand up to him. At first he was angry, but when he saw that Tracy meant it when she said she was calling the police, he backed off. When Tracy finally left, he didn't put up a fight at all.

We talked a little bit about setting goals when we discussed creating confidence. However, this is such an important skill that it bears further discussion.

Setting goals is both an art and a science. It is about finding what speaks to your soul and then figuring out the most logical way to turn that dream into reality.

Even if you think you know what fuels your passions, it is always good to explore all the possibilities life might have in store for you. After all, how will you ever know if you have a deep love of sewing if you never try sewing lessons?

Before you set your goals, spend a little time trying to determine where you want to go in life and what types of activities you want to pursue.

Inspiration for Your Goals

If you can't get beyond the basic, "I want to save up enough to retire" goals, it is time to look outside of yourself for some inspiration. Here are some of my favorite techniques for getting the creative juices flowing:

- **Pick Up a New Book:** If you generally read fiction, try non-fiction. If you love gardening books, try a spiritual guide instead. Spend an afternoon at the library. Go to a few different sections and pull off some books to flip through. Read the first few pages to see if it speaks to you. You might just find that you take home a couple of books that are completely different from your normal reading fare.

- **Listen to New Lectures:** Just like the books you read, you can get stuck in a rut with lectures as well.

You may only listen to one speaker or one style of talks. There is nothing wrong with having your favorite, but it can be helpful to change things a bit. It is important to remember that lectures can impact our mood in a profound way. If you always listen to slow, depressing talks, there is a very good chance that you may find you are always feeling a bit blue. Change the topic with some upbeat talks instead.

- **Break Out of Old Habits:** It is easy to act a certain way because 'that's the way it's always been done.' You always drive to work via a certain route. You always have the coffee and bagel for breakfast. You always watch TV at 8pm; break up your routine to inspire a little out of the box thinking.

- **Drop Self-Imposed Limitations:** Is there a little voice in the back of your head telling you what you can and cannot do? Does it tell you that you can't go back to school because you are over 40? Does it say that you can't grow your own vegetables because a black thumb runs in your family? If you constantly hear yourself saying you can't do something before you've even tried, it is time to banish the negative talk and introduce some positive thinking.

Once you have expanded your horizons and experimented with some different forms of inspiration, it is time to put those newfound interests into action.

Goal-Setting 101

The process of finding inspiration is the art of goal-setting; now let's get into the science of it. This is where the rubber meets the road and you put it into action plans that will take you to the next level of life.

The first step is to take stock of where you are in terms of your interests. Ask yourself:

- What skills do I have?
- What skills do I need?
- Where can I go to attain those skills?
- Do I know people who can help me?
- What other options do I have for pursuing this interest?

Let's look at an example...let's say you have a trendy teen who is into clothes, but your wallet just can't keep up with her trips to the mall. Rather than cut her off, you decide you would like to learn to sew clothes to supplement her wardrobe. So where do you start? You don't start by running out and buying a top of the line machine and oodles of fabric. Instead, you start by considering whether you have any sewing experience. If so, do you have experience sewing the type of clothes your daughter likes?

No? Then it is time to consider where you can get those skills. You could take a class at a local store. Or you could ask your aunt who sews to help you get started; she might also have fabric and notions you could borrow.

Sewing is an easy example, but the same process can be used for any goal, no matter how large or small. Whether you want to go back to school, open a business or travel the world, you can take a big idea and turn it into an easily managed series of steps.

All these questions as well as your options must be carefully considered to make your goal-setting effective. After all, there is goal-setting and there is smart goal-setting. The difference between the two is that smart goal-setting involves taking small, attainable steps that not only save you time, but also money.

Create Deadlines

Another important aspect of goal-setting is creating deadlines. So many people have grand ambitions, but never reach them because it is too easy to put off their plans until 'later.' However, later never comes, and their dreams remain unrealized.

It isn't enough to create a vague time frame. Think about all those New Year's resolutions you've made throughout the years. You were going to lose weight this year, write your novel, or begin a new career. It was only a matter of time before November rolled around, and you weren't any closer to reaching your goal than you were in January.

After you've created your steps, you need to attach a deadline to each one. If you want to go back to school, give yourself a deadline to contact the school admissions office. Write it on your calendar and tell yourself that this is a date written in stone. If your deadline rolls around and you haven't taken action yet, you'd better be sure that it is on your to-do list for that day.

Focus on Multiple Goals to Stay Motivated

It is easy to get burned out if you are living and breathing one particular dream day in and day out. Variety is the spice of life and working towards multiple goals can help keep you feeling inspired.

Select a goal for each facet of your life – work, family and personal development. As you create steps for your goals, spread them out so you are working towards each goal each month. When you start to get burned out on planning for your business, you can spend some time unwinding by working towards your hobby or craft goal.

As a domestic abuse survivor, you may still be working on getting your self-confidence and self-esteem back. If so, the idea of working towards one goal – let alone multiple goals – may be overwhelming. That's understandable, but don't let it stop you!

We are often our own worst enemies. In an effort to be safe and avoid failure, we often underestimate our own abilities:

"You miss 100% of the shots you never take."
Wayne Gretzky

This quote from hockey great, Wayne Gretzky is a great reminder that you will never achieve anything unless you try. Of course there is a chance you might fail; that comes with the territory of having dreams.

It can help to imagine the worst that could happen if you fail. If you try applying for a new job and you don't get it, what then? You would probably be disappointed, but the world wouldn't come screeching to a halt. No, instead you would actually be better prepared for the next job application.

The temptation is to take failures as a personal reflection on you. In other words, we often think that I didn't succeed so I must be a worthless loser. Well, I am here to tell you that it is time to toss the negative talk!

Replace those self-defeating thoughts with a new positive outlook. Consider them as opportunities to improve. If you lose out on a promotion, evaluate what you could do differently next time. Maybe it was outside your control – the result of office politics or unfair favoritism. In that case, realize that the decision had nothing to do with you, and you can feel good knowing you did your very best.

Putting It into Action

____ Take a skills assessment. If you are looking for a job, a temp agency might complete one for you. Otherwise, you can search online for a number of different self-assessment tools.

____ Do some extra reading. Books such as, *'What Color is Your Parachute?'* walk you through self-discovery exercises that can help you identify and create meaningful goals.

____ Write down 3 short-term goals that you can achieve this week. Then reach them.

____ Write down 3 long-term goals that may take months or more to reach. Then, during the next month, take the first step towards achieving them.

____ Share at least one of your long-term goals with a friend who can help keep you accountable and on track to reaching it.

Chapter 6

Live on a Budget

"There came a time when the risk to remain tight in the bud was more painful than the risk it took to blossom."
Anais Nin

Domestic violence was something that never even crossed my mind growing up. Born and raised in a white suburban neighborhood, I always thought it was one of those things that happened only in the movies or maybe the inner city.

My husband was absolutely charming when I met him. I fell head over heels in love. After we got married, we moved to a nearby town, and I commuted to my office job.

Changes in my husband's behavior started subtly enough. First, he started asking me all sorts of questions about work – who I had lunch with, what they were wearing. I thought it was strange, but decided I was being silly.

Then he started hinting I should leave work. We didn't have kids so it didn't make sense to me, but he thought there was no reason I should work when he could support us both. It seemed like a nice gesture, but I wanted to keep working.

My husband wouldn't drop it, and then one day, he showed up at the office. He accused me of having an affair with my boss and created this huge scene. I was so embarrassed that I quit the next week.

Around the same time, I lost access to our bank accounts. I used to be able to check them online, but one day my password wouldn't work. When I asked my husband about it, he said that the bank had an online security issue, and he needed to change it. When I asked for the new one, he made me feel guilty for asking and then changed the subject.

I probably should have pushed the subject, but I didn't. Inside all these warning sirens were going off, but my husband was a master manipulator. Everything was put back on me. Eventually, I began to believe him. When I tried to bring it up with friends, they brushed it off too. My husband put on a good show, and everyone thought he was perfect.

I lived like this for 9 years with him controlling my every move. My car was eventually sold (we couldn't afford it, my husband said), and I spent most of my time at home alone. When I finally got up the courage to leave, I had no clue how much my husband made, where our money was and how I would pay for an attorney.

Fortunately, the women's shelter in a nearby town was amazing. They helped me and eventually, we discovered that my husband had a six figure salary.

It took years for me to realize that my husband was abusing me. I only wish I had learned that earlier. He did such a number on my self-esteem and confidence – I feel like I am still healing, 3 years later.

Finances are one of the main reasons many women choose to stay in abusive relationships. As outlined previously, abusers like to isolate their victims. They force them to quit jobs and cut ties with the outside world. Financially abusive spouses may control all aspects of the household money.

For women escaping from such a situation, the prospects of successfully starting over their lives can be daunting. With no job, no money and perhaps limited financial skills, the idea that they can support themselves financially may seem like a fairy tale. Unfortunately, many women in this situation choose to stay with their abusive husband rather than risk leaving this situation.

If you are in an abusive situation right now, do not let money hold you back. You can leave your abuser and still make ends meet. No, it may not be easy at first, but there are some amazing groups out there that work with victims of domestic violence.

These groups can help you locate housing, learn new skills and find a job. In addition, they will be able to help you navigate the process of applying for child support and possibly alimony as well. They can help you get back on your feet and start you on a path to self-sufficiency, which will ensure that you never again become trapped in an abusive situation. To find a support organization in your area, call the Domestic Violence Hotline: 1-800-799-SAFE (7233).

For those who have already left their abuser, you may be feeling overwhelmed by the prospect of budgeting for the first time or managing family finances on your own. I promise you – it's not that hard! In this chapter, we will review some tips that will make managing your money easy and simple.

Earn Some Cash

Even if you already have a job or have found a new one, chances are you will need some extra cash. You may have to hire an attorney if you are getting a divorce, or you may have moving expenses. It is not unusual for abusers to hide money so you may not have any savings or perhaps there is a large amount of debt in your name.

In addition, there can be a delay in receiving child support payments and some men are notorious about doing everything in their power to manipulate the system and get out of supporting their children. It is best not to count on child support until there is a track record of the payments coming on time.

So with all that in mind, the first thing to do after leaving an abusive situation is to store up some extra money. If you have a job, put part of your paycheck into savings for an emergency fund. Otherwise, you need to start bringing in some cash to not only pay for daily expenses, but also be prepared for extra expenses that may come up as you branch out on your own.

Some options for earning quick money include:

- Sell items on eBay, half.com or Craig's list.
- Sell items at a local pawn shop.
- Baby-sit for friends and neighbors.
- House or pet sit.
- Put a hobby to use by making something to sell. Ask local businesses to stock your items or sell online through eBay or etsy.com.
- Hold a yard sale.
- Return any recent purchases that you still have the receipt for.
- Take any scrap metal you can find to a recycling center.
- Deliver newspapers.

Leaving a relationship can be either difficult or refreshing, you make the choice. Rather than dwelling on the fact that you need to get rid of some stuff to make ends meet, look at it as a change to completely reinvent yourself. This is your opportunity to start over fresh with no baggage and no false expectations from others.

After all, why would you want to hold on to the jewelry given to you by a man who abused and berated you for years? Go to the jewelry store or the pawn shop and make some money off those items!

As you establish your new household, take careful stock of all you own. Does something remind you of your ex? Are there items you own only because your ex thought you should have them? For example, maybe your closet is filled with items that he bought you, but they really aren't your style. Move them out!

This is not only a process of making money; it is also a healing process. One in which you let go of those bad emotions and memories and begin anew. You are living for yourself now!

Beef Up Your Savings

Once you have a positive cash flow, you need to allocate some of that money to an account. As mentioned previously, there may be some expenses associated with a divorce or establishing your own household. It is good to have money set aside to pay for those items. However, it is also important to be prepared for the emergencies that will undoubtedly crop up from time to time. The car's transmission might go out or your roof may spring a leak. Whatever it is, you want to be prepared without having to resort to racking up credit card debt or borrowing from friends and family.

As a good rule of thumb, you should start with at least $1,000 in savings if you have debt. Saving $1,000 might seem like a high mountain to climb if you are only making minimum wage, but it can be done. If you sell some items or hold a yard sale, you'll find yourself with a nice pot of money to start your account with. Then set aside $10, $20 or more each week until you reach your goal. Once you have saved the $1,000, it is time to knock out your debt, but we'll talk about that in a moment.

For those of you without any debt (good for you!), you will want to start saving for a larger emergency fund. Financial experts say you should have enough to cover 3 to 6 months worth of expenses.

How do you know whether to save up for 3 months or 6 months? Well, a lot of that depends on your personal comfort level. If you were a victim of financial abuse, you may feel a little more comfortable with a bigger safety net. If 6 months worth of money in the bank helps you sleep better at night, then there's your answer. On the other hand, if you have a stable job and feel like you could easily find a new one if laid-off, then you may only need the 3 months worth of expenses.

Again, these are just expenses we're talking about. If your gross income is $2,000 a month, but you only have $1,500 in monthly expenses, that's the figure you use to calculate how much to save. When calculating expenses don't forget to include: utilities, gas, food, housing, and any debt payments.

Set Financial Goals

Your budget is a roadmap to your financial future. Before you sit down to draw up the map, you need to know where you are going. When you set financial goals, it is okay to dream big. Think about all the things you would like to do that involve money.

Financial goals may be to:
> o Put your children through college.
> o Retire early.
> o Travel the country or the world.
> o Start a business.
> o Work from home.
> o Buy a house and pay it off.

After you've created a list of goals, you need to prioritize them. Consider which items speak to you the most. The ones that inspire the most passion should move to the top of your list.

Also consider the time frame for each goal. If you want to travel, there is no set time for that to happen. However, if you want to help your daughter pay for college and she's 10, you only have about 8 years to reach that goal. Give the time-sensitive goals priority.

Create Your Budget

Now we are to the meat of your financial planning. It is time to make a budget. For some people, the mere word 'budget' can strike fear into their hearts. It seems constricting, complicated and joyless. Others find budgets fascinating; they love working with numbers and can spend hours moving figures around to find the ultimate spending plan.

Whichever camp you fall into, a budget is essential for running your household smoothly and reaching your financial goals. If the idea of a budget seems too confining, then think of it as your permission to spend money. A budget doesn't mean you can't buy something, it just means that you have planned your buying in advance.

For example, let's say you love a bargain and can't wait to hit the garage sales in the spring. A budget doesn't mean you have to sit home every Saturday morning; instead, it means that you tell yourself I have $40 to spend at sales this month and when the money is gone, I am done shopping. Budgeting certainly has an element of self-control to it, but it does not entail depriving yourself of everything you might want.

So let's get started! The first thing you need to do is track your spending for a month. That means you save every single receipt and write down every penny you spend…right down to the 75 cents that went into the vending machine during your lunch break.

This can be the most tedious part of budgeting, but it is very important. Please don't skip it! Not only does tracking your expenses help you make a realistic budget, it also identifies holes in your budget where money may be "leaking."

Work lunches are a common budget leak. Once you realize how much all those drive through meals and trips to the vending machine add up, you may be motivated to start packing a lunch. Plugging budget holes leaves extra money that can then be used to reach your financial goals, create a savings safety net or buy something you really want.

At the end of the month, tally all your expenses; break them down into categories that make sense to you and pull out a clean sheet of paper. Time to do your budget!

At the top of your paper, write your income. This can be from your job, any cash assistance you receive from the state and child support. As I mentioned earlier, I don't recommend planning for child support unless you have already been receiving it on a regular basis. The sad truth is that many men – particularly those who have been abusive – bristle at the idea that they should pay you anything. They will often do everything in their power to avoid paying child support. Don't include those payments in your budget planning until they are well established.

Although some people like to use their gross income, for the sake of simplicity, I recommend planning your budget with your net income. This is the amount of money you bring home in your paycheck each week after taxes and other expenses are taken out.

Now create a column with your fixed expenses. Fixed expenses are the ones that you pay each month. Usually, a fixed expense will be the same amount each month although they can vary, as in the case of utilities.

Your fixed expenses may include:

- Rent

- Gas
- Utilities – Electric, Heat, Telephone, Water, Trash
- Daycare
- Debt Payments – Credit Cards, Personal Loans, etc.
- Food
- Monthly Insurance Payments - health insurance

To make planning for fixed expenses easier, call your utility companies and ask if they offer a budget plan. Utilities that offer budget plans estimate your total monthly usage and charge you a fixed monthly rate. If you go over their estimate, you may have to pay a little extra in the spring, but that sure beats having a $350 heating bill in December.

After your fixed expenses, it is time to think about your variable expenses. These are the items that don't necessarily come up every month, but you still expect to pay for them over the course of the year. Do your best to estimate how many these items cost you on a *yearly* basis and write those numbers down.

Variable expenses may include:
- Auto Maintenance
- Auto Registration
- Back to School Shopping
- Insurance Payments Made Quarterly or Annually
- Gifts Spending
- Vacation Expenses
- Clothing
- Hair Cuts
- Household Repair

Number crunchers and budget fans may want to keep each of these items in separate categories and track them individually. If that sounds like fun, I am not going to stand in your way. But for everyone else, let's simplify the process of saving and paying for variable expenses.

Add up all your variable expenses and divide by 12. This will tell you how much money you need to set aside each month to pay for them. If you expect to pay $3,600 for the year, you need to include $300 in your monthly budget to pay for your variable expenses. I recommend starting a separate account to hold this money so it doesn't get mixed in with your emergency savings.

If the amount of money you need for emergency expenses seems staggering, you may need to scale back your vacation or holiday plans. While we are lumping all the variable expenses into one category for monthly budgeting purposes, you should still have a target amount for each category; that way when you go shopping for gifts, you know exactly how much you can spend without breaking the bank.

Once you have your fixed expenses and monthly variable expense payment figured it is time to see if you can actually meet your monthly obligations.

Add up all the expenses and subtract them from your income. If you have money left over, congratulations! You can allocate that money to your savings or financial goals. If you come up short, you need to rework your numbers. Maybe you could car pool to work or pack lunches. Clothing expenses could be scaled back or you may need to shop around for cheaper insurance.

If there is no way you can pare down your expenses, you need to look at how you can increase your income. Spread the word to family and friends that you are available to baby-sit or work odd jobs. In addition, go through your belongings and see what you can sell to bring in extra cash.

Your budget should spend every dollar you have incoming. Without a plan for that money, there is a good chance that it will be wasted. You may have to play with the numbers to get them just right, but in the end, you will have a workable budget.

Your final plan should look something like this:

Monthly Income

$2196 – Work

Monthly Expenses

$650 – Rent
$105 – Utilities
$125 – Car Insurance
$50 –   Gas
$450 – Daycare
$400 – Food
$250 – Variable Expenses
$125 – College Fund
$41 - Savings

$2196 – Total

See how the total of the expenses equals the total income? You can customize the categories however you want. Maybe you want to have $50 in 'fun money' every month that you can spend as you want. If travel is one of your financial goals, you can make that category too. The point is that you create a budget that acts as a roadmap for where you want your money to take you.

Cut Up the Credit Cards

Nothing is more detrimental to your financial success than debt. It sucks up valuable spending power and creates a cycle of dependency. You just got out of one bad relationship – don't start a new one with a bank or credit card company!

If you don't have debt right now, avoid it by anticipating expenses. If your car is 10 years old, start putting money aside each month to offset the purchase price of a new one. In addition, having a well-funded emergency fund is one of the best defenses against debt. When disaster strikes, you will be prepared to meet it head-on.

However, if you are like most American families, you probably already have some debt. As you prepare your budget, look at how much money goes each month to pay back your debt obligations. Wouldn't it be nice to have the money available to spend on other things?

Make an effort to get out of debt as quickly as possible. Once you have $1,000 in savings, send any extra money you make to pay off your smallest debt. Once you pay off that debt, take the money you were sending there and concentrate it on the next smallest payment. Eventually, this 'debt snowball' will build steam and quickly wipe out what you owe.

Putting It into Action

___ Start keeping a monthly log of all your expenses.

___ Gather up information on your income and other sources of revenue.

___ Brainstorm your financial goals.

___ Create a basic budget.

___ Identify 3 ways you can make extra money this month.

___ Write a list of debts or other priorities so you can easily route any extra money you receive to the appropriate place.

___ Cut up your credit cards.

Chapter 7

Manage Your Time

"Manage your time, before you regret your time."
Zohra Sarwari

I moved fast after meeting my husband. We were married less than 3 months after we met. My parents said we were going too fast, but my husband said that when you're in love, you're in love.

The first year was nice. I have good memories of that time. On our anniversary, we didn't do much to celebrate. I mentioned that it was a bit of a letdown, and my husband punched me in the arm.

The punch surprised me, but I didn't think of it as abusive. After all, he hadn't hit me in the face or anything like that. Too bad, it didn't end there.

My husband started playing mind games with me. He would sulk around the house and when I asked what was wrong, I was accused of reading too much into his behavior. Every few months, for no good reason, he would hit me. Usually, it was because he didn't like something I said, but it was always over dumb stuff.

One time, he pulled my hair and kicked me because I commented that the dishes never seem to get done. I wasn't criticizing him. I only meant that it seems like there are always dishes to wash. He took it as me giving him a hard time and attacked me. Another time he threw me to the ground and spat on me because I said I was late for work and couldn't help him find his wallet.

The bruises were always where I could cover them – on my thighs and upper arms. I never went swimming in the summer.

My husband told me I was fat and ugly. He said that I made him hit me because of my behavior. He said that I was lucky to have him because no other man would want such an ugly, bloated wife.

A couple of times I mentioned going to marriage counseling. My husband became enraged at the suggestion. He told me that we were married, and no one needed to know anything about our problems.

The last time he punched me, we were on our way to a party. Looking at everyone else and seeing how happy they were, I knew I could do better. And even if I couldn't, anything had to be an improvement over living with this miserable man.

I went to see a church pastor the next week. I told him everything. He gave me his blessing to get a divorce. I packed up and moved in with my mum the next day.

My husband left me messages and sent notes asking for a second chance. As far as I am concerned, he had plenty of chances and blew them all.

As a newly independent woman, managing your time may be just as difficult as managing your money. It is not unusual for battered women to spend years isolated at home, doing only housework or what their husbands told them. Now that you are free from your abusive spouse, you have a lot more freedom... and responsibilities.

When you are managing your time wisely, there is no reason why you can't do your work, keep your house in order and spend time with the kids or enjoy your own pursuits. Time management is an art, and everyone needs to find the system that works for them. However, here are some pointers to help you get started:

Time Management Tools

To effectively manage your time, you need to be able to track your tasks and daily events. There are all sorts of tools out there to track your time:

o Planners
o Calendars
o Email Calendars
o iPhone Apps
o Online Programs

Like budgeting, some folks adore time management. There are entire stores dedicated to planning your time. You can use whatever system strikes your fancy, but all you really need is a monthly calendar and a blank sheet of paper.

Time Management Basics

If you are single or have few time commitments, you can use a monthly calendar to record all your one-time events. These can be school events, doctor appointments or dates with friends. If you regularly have two or more events on any given day, you will probably want to upgrade to a daily planner.

Planners can be large or small, but they provide you with more space to record multiple events, as well as details such as phone numbers, directions or other notes. Many planners also have space for to-do lists which can consolidate your paperwork.

Otherwise, you can use a blank sheet of paper for your to-do list. Sit down in the evening before bed and think about everything that needs to get done the next day. This could be events, house chores, work obligations or hobbies.

You will find that much of your to-do list will repeat every day. After all, the dishes will always need to be done, and dinner needs to get to the table each night. To save time, you can create a template that includes daily tasks as well as spaces for one-time events. You can use the computer to make the template or you can write one by hand and make photocopies.

A sample to-do list template might be:

To-Do List

___ Make Beds
___ Plan/Make Dinner
___ Do Dishes
___ Check Homework
___ Do Laundry
___ Sort Mail
___ Read

___ _____
___ _____
___ _____
___ _____
___ _____

As you complete each task, you check off the item. In the blank spaces, you can write whatever extra needs to be done that day. For example, you could add grocery shopping, gardening or paying bills to your list.

This is nothing fancy. It is, however, a simple and easy way to start managing your time effectively. Over time, you can adjust your time management process as you discover what works for you and what doesn't.

Some women discover that they like having their entire day mapped out. If you like having designated times for each task, you will definitely want a daily planner that is broken down by hours. Then you can assign each task a specific time. For example, you can plan that 1pm-2pm is your reading time or that 4pm is when you start dinner.

A Square Peg in a Round Hole

As with budgeting, you need to be a realist when it comes to time management. If you know you always like to watch TV for an hour at night, don't plan to clean the bathroom at that time. Likewise, if you do better on the fly, it is not wise to try to box yourself in by using a rigid hour-by-hour schedule.

There may be a period of self-discovery with time management and that is to be expected. Pay attention to your energy levels: are you ready to go first thing in the morning or do you peak in the afternoon? Try to mix up when you schedule tasks to find out what is the optimal time for each duty.

As you learn your own natural rhythms, you can determine when best to do your work. If you like watching TV at night, you can fold laundry while sitting on the couch. Maybe you discover that getting outside for a walk first thing in the morning makes your whole day more productive. Or it could be that you are a night owl.

The point is there is no right or wrong answer to how you schedule your time. Each individual is unique and what works for your friend may not work for you. That doesn't mean you can't give her system a try. It just means that if you find it's not working, you move on to something else. Don't try to force a square peg into a round hole.

The Art of Saying No

To be truly effective at time management, you must learn to say no. You will never have smooth days if you are constantly dropping everything to accommodate someone else's needs. This can be difficult, especially for battered women who are used to be on the receiving end of abuse when they refuse a request.

When declining someone's request – whether it be to chair a school event or watch the neighbor's kids – remember to be polite but firm. A simple way to say 'no' is:

'Thank you for thinking of me. However, I have other plans and can't commit to this right now.'

If they persist, you don't need to explain yourself, repeat:

'I wish I could help, but this isn't a good time for me. I'm sorry.'

Anyone who badgers you further lacks manners, and you should excuse yourself from their presence as quickly as possible.

That said; keep in mind the particular circumstances of the situation. If your next door neighbor is constantly asking you to watch her son, don't hesitate to say no. However, if a friend is calling for the first time and sounds a bit desperate for help, sometimes it pays to be flexible. Remember that part of being a good friend is being there in a time of need.

If you can't help with a request, you can soften your 'no' by offering alternatives. Recommend a good sitter to your neighbor or consider helping with the school fundraiser set-up if you don't want to be a part of the planning committee.

In the end, the best way to ensure your time is not being sabotaged is to ask yourself why you are saying 'yes' to a commitment. Is it because it is something you enjoy? Or are you doing it out of guilt and obligation? If it's the latter, don't allow yourself to be bullied or manipulated. You've allowed others to dictate your life for too long, haven't you? It's time to say 'no' and then stand your ground.

Prioritize Your Tasks

There comes a time when everyone will realize that there are just not enough hours in the day to get everything done. If you feel stretched out and frazzled at the end of the day, it may be time to take a second look at your to-do list.

Start by considering whether you can eliminate any non-essential tasks. Let's say you volunteer in your child's classroom once a week. You could free up time by asking the teacher if you could switch to every other week or once a month. The same can be done for any committees or boards you sit on. If you do not love these volunteer commitments, consider dropping them. Time is valuable, and you should focus yours on the projects and tasks most important to you.

"To make every moment count, use it."
Zohra Sarwari

In addition to dropping tasks that are not necessary or meaningful to you, look for ways to stretch the hours you have. Grouping tasks together can increase your efficiency. Make all your phone calls at one time and run errands together.

Also, take advantage of idle time that could be put to good use. If you have to pick up your son from practice, bring along a book to read or organize coupons while you wait. If possible, use public transportation whenever possible. Not only does that save you money, it also frees up time. Rather than driving, you can spend your commute time doing something more productive.

Putting It into Action

____ Select a time management system to try out. Are you a techie? Look for a phone app or online calendar. More old school? Try a paper calendar or planner.

____ Determine whether you will plan your day loosely or schedule tasks by the hour.

____ Keep a 'time journal' for at least a week. Keep notes in your planner, if you are using one, regarding your time management and energy levels. Are you feeling sluggish in the afternoon? Do you have trouble getting through a certain task? After a week, review your notes and determine whether changes should be made to your schedule.

____ Review your schedule to ensure that you have set aside time for yourself and your interests.

____ Role play saying 'no' with a friend until you feel comfortable turning down requests for your time.

Chapter 8

Live Your Life to the Fullest!

"People are like stained-glass windows.
They sparkle and shine when the sun is out,
but when the darkness sets in, their true beauty is
revealed...only if there is a light from within."
Elizabeth Kübler-Ross

You are a strong woman; there is no doubt about that. You have experienced pain that no one should ever have to endure. As I said at the beginning of this book, I hope you have already left your abuser. No one deserves to be treated like an object or a possession. You are worth more.

In case you are still in that relationship, I want to share two last stories with you. The first one is particularly heartbreaking because it shows a child's view of domestic violence:

My parents fought for as long as I could remember. My Mom would sometimes yell at my Dad, but usually it was Dad who went over the edge. He would kick, scream and punch all of us. Once he put us kids in a closet and threatened to kill Mom with a knife. I can close my eyes and remember that day like it was yesterday.

If I didn't do the dishes right, I was slapped. My brother was punched in the neck once because he forgot the trash. We would avoid Dad at all costs. We were always scared that he was going to go off the deep end.

When I hit my teen years, things got worse. Dad started going through my room. He found a love letter from a boy I liked and went into a tirade. At dinner time, he forced me to eat everything on my plate. Once I got sick and threw up. I was made to eat my vomit since Dad was sure I had done it on purpose. To this day, I have trouble eating, and I've struggled with eating disorders for years.

At age 16, I went to live with my Grandma. She was my hero. After all that went on at home, it was like a dream to live with someone who didn't call me names or pull my hair.

After college, I got married. Ended up, I chose someone just like Dad. He drank and beat me once a week. I spent 2 years with him before deciding that enough was enough. I am getting better now, but it still hurts to think of all the people who were suppose to love me and instead abused me.

Not only is this story tragic because of the abuse this girl endured at the hands of her father, but it is a reminder of how violence cycles through families. As a mother, you model for your children how a marriage should be. If your daughter sees you being abused and berated by your husband, she will expect no better for herself.

If you have a daughter, think long and hard before staying in an unhealthy relationship. Is this what you want for your daughter? Do you want her to think that men hitting women is okay? Do you want her to think that the wife is a doormat that a husband walks all over? Do you want her to grow up and make the same painful mistakes?

Now let's look at a final story:

I grew up in a physically abusive home and was sure that I would never put myself in the same situation as my Mom.

So it was ironic that one morning I woke up and realized that I was married to an abusive man. No, he didn't beat me, but called me names, sexually abused me and withheld money. I had never heard of financial abuse until someone told me that what my husband did with our money was the definition of financial abuse.

Throughout our marriage, his behavior got worse and worse. The name calling increased – I hated going to bed because he constantly forced himself on me. Eventually, my nerves were frayed, and I was hospitalized for attempted suicide. I made two return trips for mentally breaking down on other occasions.

Of course, while I was in the hospital, my husband was a model citizen; very concerned and constantly by my side. Everyone thought he was very sweet and caring…no one had a clue he put me there.

After I was hospitalized, I started to egg my husband on, hoping he would hit me. In my mind, once he hit me, it could rightfully be called abuse, and I could leave. While deep in my heart, I knew he was already abusing me, I didn't feel like it was a big enough problem to leave.

We did separate for a year, but I eventually went back. I don't know why. I guess I wanted to believe that he had changed. Also, I didn't know how to manage the money and never had enough to pay my bills. However, it was never any different. He was the same old guy, except now I think he knew that my threats to leave were all empty.

What I feel worse about is my son. He got married two years ago and treats his wife the same way my husband treats me. I tried to talk to him once and he hit me. My own son hit me!

Not only is my husband an abusive man, but my son is too. I wish I had made different decisions earlier. It is too late for me, but not for other women. Get out, especially if you have children. They are innocent and don't deserve the abuse.

While I disagree with this woman's assessment that it is too late for her (it is never too late!), I do think her story is a poignant reminder of how our actions extend beyond ourselves. Like the previous story, the abuse she endured cycled from one relationship to another. Except instead of placing her daughter in an abusive relationship, it created an abusive son.

Now that you have read this guide to healing, you are ready to start the next great adventure of your life. It is time to live life to the fullest! Life may not always be easy, but it can certainly be rewarding.

Once you have freed yourself of the shackles of abuse, it is time to spread your wings and soar to new heights. As author and philosopher, Henry David Thoreau said, *"We must suck the marrow out of life."*

To help make sure you don't miss a moment of living, consider these:

Start a Journal: Perhaps nothing is more revealing than putting our deepest thoughts on paper. Journaling can help deal with the trauma of abuse or sort out your emotions. It can also be a safe place to flesh out your hopes, dreams and goals.

Forgive Yourself: If you've been in an abusive relationship for an extended period of time, your self-esteem is probably already at an all-time low. There is no use beating yourself up over lost time and past mistakes. Remember The Lion King? Hakuna Matata! The past is behind you. Don't let dwelling on yesterday distract you from making tomorrow a better day.

Love Yourself: Likewise, always, always remember that you are worthy of love and respect. If someone treats you badly, it says more about them than it does about you. No one can take away your self-worth. If you take away nothing else from this book, I hope it is that.

Never Stop Improving Yourself: We are all works in progress. Don't settle for second best. Spend every day trying to reach your potential. Sure, you will stumble and fall, but that is part of living. Get up, wipe yourself off and start over again. You will be better for the experience.

Look for the Good in Life: If you focus on the negative aspects of life, your days will be long and miserable. Truly joyful people have tunnel vision when it comes to happiness. There is no way anyone is going to rain on their parade!

Surround Yourself With Positive People: Positivity feeds off positivity. All those good feelings are contagious. Make a point to seek out happy people and associate with them as often as possible.

As you walk through this journey of life, don't expect perfection. Remember that failure and imperfection are a part of life. You will never erase them from your world. However, what you can change is how you react to those difficult times in life. You can choose to let them throw you into depression and despair or you can see them as opportunities to improve yourself or try something new. In other words, you can have lemons or you can make lemonade.

It can be difficult to change how you react to life's challenges. With practice, you will find that looking on the sunny side comes naturally to you.

I invite you to live life fully and completely – don't wait another minute – start today!

"Live by example and always check your intentions."
Zohra Sarwari

Putting It into Action

___ Start a journal. If you prefer to type instead of writing longhand, you can make an electronic journal through a computer word processing program.

___ Practice gratitude; each night, write down 5 things that make you feel blessed or grateful.

___ Evaluate friendships; avoid "toxic" friends and seek out positive people.

___ Give yourself permission to fail. Life will not always be a bowl of cherries. Learn to take the good with the bad and use all life's experiences to better yourself.

In conclusion, it's time to be the woman you were born to be. Don't settle for less, make every moment count, remember the blessings of Allaah (God the Almighty), and be thankful.

Have You Booked
Zohra Sarwari

The Ideal Professional Speaker for Your Next Event!

"Zohra Sarwari was very ENGAGING and successfully CAPTIVATED her audience. She was able to present visuals and demonstrated knowledge of her materials. At the end, she was encircled by students who wanted to talk to her and to purchase her books."

Catherine Rue
Student Life Administrator
Northampton Community College

"Zohra is one of the most relevant speakers I have ever heard. She takes a very serious topic and makes it easy to understand. The information Zohra provides is very timely and purposeful. I am sure your audience will appreciate her approach and effective delivery. Thanks for shedding some light on my world as well."

Stan Pearson II, MBA
Author - Speaker - Radio Personality

Zohra Sarwari's 9 Books:

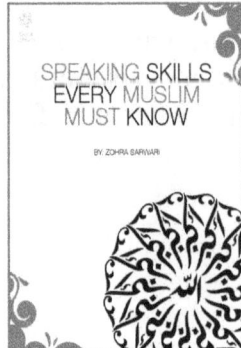

Zohra Sarwari's Inspirational E-books:

Have You Bought The Series "Things Every Kid Should Know: Smoking, Drugs, Alcohol and Bullying" for Your Kids?

Written By A
"10 Year Old" Muslim Author,
Alya Nuri

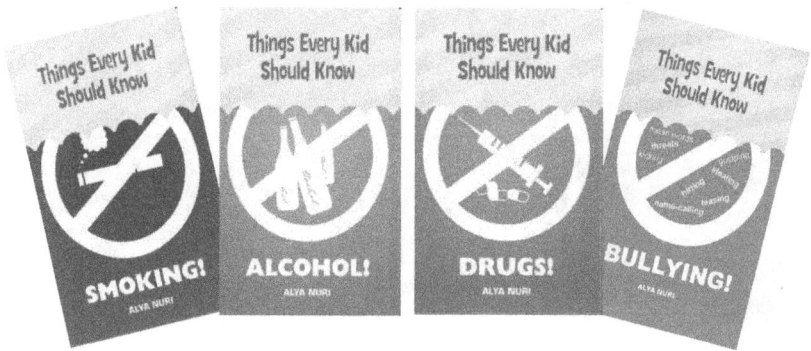

Have You Bought The Series "Things Every Kid Should Know: Strangers and Fire!" for Your Kids?

Written By A
"6 Year Old" Muslim Author,
Zafar Nuri